SEASCAPES

DIYA NARAYAN

Made with ♥ on the Notion Press Platform
www.notionpress.com

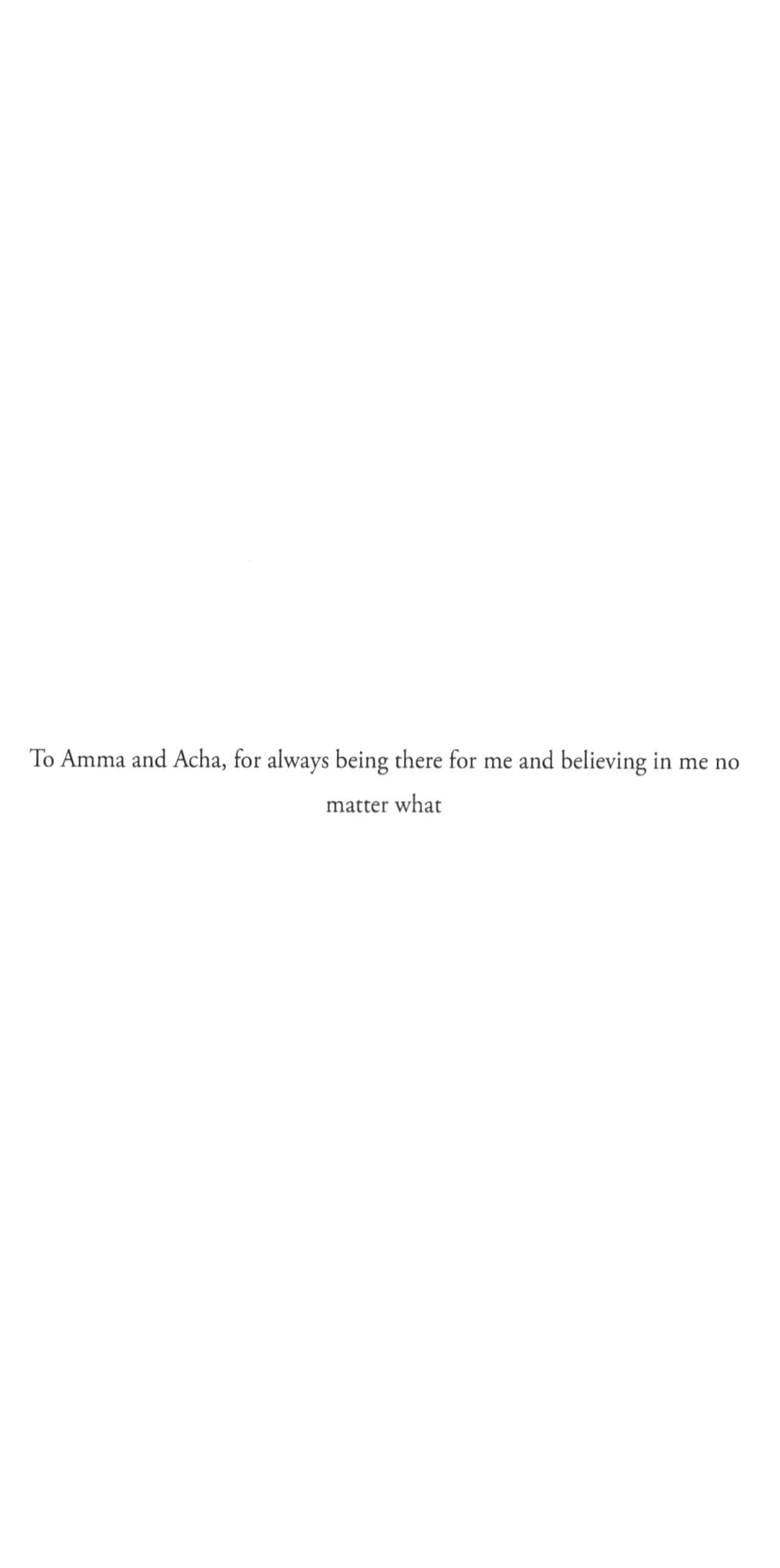
To Amma and Acha, for always being there for me and believing in me no matter what

Contents

Foreword

Seascapes has been a work in progress from the day I began to write. It was in 2018 that I had decided I wanted to publish, not being satisfied with my work and with many fears in my mind it took a backseat. Eventually in 2022 I started an official instagram for all my poems, and called it Seascapes. The name seascapes comes from my love for the ocean, something that is reflected in most of my poems. At the same time, seascapes is more than just about sea, it is full of all my life experiences painted with the metaphor of the sea. This is just the begining, the sunrise over the horizon, and may the sun never set on *Seascapes*.

Acknowledgements

I would like to thank my English teachers, all of them that encouraged me to write and believed in me when I dreamed of being a writer.
I would like to thank my family, who have had relentless faith and belief in me.
I would like to thank all my friends, who alongside some of my darkest moments, never let me lose hope.
I would like to thank myself, for taking the first step in my adventures of writing.

1. Saltwater Lullaby

Home

Home is the smell of Seabreeze,

Home is letting my body float in the open ocean.

Home is crying at the shores of unfamiliar beaches.

Home is hoping to drown but learning to swim.

2

I feel the need for a break.

Away from it all,

I yearn to sit on the shores of an unnamed beach,

Thinking of nothing but how the waves collapse into one another,

Creating the perfect balance and sound.

The sound that is music to my ears.

The sound that makes me forget that there is a world beyond these shores.

The sound that plays in my head everytime I close my eyes.

3

No matter my age,

or my tenure,

I will always feel like a child when I am put on the shore of a beach.

Barely able to keep the excitement in,

Eager to feel the waves hit my body.

I never care that the water hurts my eyes,

I keep them wide open anyway.

I always wish to be as close to the ocean as physically possible,

and sometimes just being in it, is not close enough.

I never feel any fear, I never have any doubts,

only a voice in my head telling me to keep swimming.

4

A world filled with wistful beaches,

waiting for a painter to capture its beauty.

Unfortunately, a poet seems to have reached the scene first:

"She is a glorious blue,

A mighty blue,

chaos flows within her,

as does love."

5

Sunsets,
walks on the beach,
leaving our footprints behind,
the sand is still stuck beneath our toes.
Our bodies in sync with the waves,
as we float, with no sense of time in our minds.
we are driven back ashore,
and giggle on our way home.
The smell of the salt on my skin does not leave,
almost as stubborn as my heart.
Leaving the place I have always felt most at home,
taking back with me,
a dark tan.

6

Crystal clear water,

heavy hearts.

We swim as if the world is weightless,

while our minds drift to every problem in the world.

we seek comfort, love and warmth,

we even manage to find it, even if it was just for a second.

7

My eyes are closed,

my feet buried in sand.

I hum along to the sound of the waves hitting each other,

a more euphoric place is not known to mankind.

I hear the jingles of an ice cream cart,

I open my eyes to see an old man selling ice candies to little kids,

all of them, beyond excited.

I smile underneath my hat,

and look back at the horizon,

the sun reflecting on the supple waves of the sea,

I let out a deep breath.

I was not in this world,

I was floating in a dream,

a dream that seemed so real,

that If I reached out I could feel the water between my fingers,

and sand beneath my toes.

8

Golden skies,

crystal clear water.

Footprints laced with memories,

empty stomachs, full hearts.

Dirty clothes and clean towels.

We were alive,

alive in a way our young minds did not know was possible.

With every breath of fresh air,

suddenly, there was no sorrow.

9

I sit here,

on the banks of this seemingly ever flowing river,

cigarette in hand,

and uncertainty written all over my forehead.

I think of all my unguided moments of grief,

even though as of this moment,

the sun shines brightly over my head,

and nothing or nobody dares hurt me.

This mind of mine,

filled with questions I cannot seem to escape,

seeking answers I do not seem to find.

I let this uncontrollable melancholy pass through my body,

as I close my eyes and feel the summer breeze slowly dry out the beads

of sweat on my forehead.

10

Sea breeze, warm sand,

and beads of sweat,

from the coasts of Kanyakumari, to the backwaters of Poovar,

my mind travels faster than my body.

My body is sat in an air conditioned car,

yet my mind is already on the seashore, and my feet are covered in

sand.

The sun continues to pierce its rays into my skin,

and I am once again transported from my living room,

to the coasts of Travancore.

As a kid when I first visited a beach, or at least the first beach visit I remember, was right after I learned to swim. I was beyond excited to test this new ability of mine where it really mattered, whether I could stay afloat in the mighty ocean or not, just ten years old but that girl was ready to swim long and far in the open ocean. I hope to carry that excitement for the rest of my life. Whenever I swim I feel like a part of me that was incomplete was put back together.

It is the same way I felt when I first swam on a beach in Goa, my father beside me, and it is the same way I feel every single time. The feeling when I glide through the water effortlessly, is a feeling so euphoric that even the poet in me can't seem to find the words to describe it.

When the saltwater touches my sunburnt skin, I feel it healing my skin. Even if the water didn't in fact heal my skin it always healed my soul. It is so easy to get lost in routine and daily life that once in a while all you need is to get lost.

Floating around for what always feels like hours but in reality is only a few seconds. The healing powers of the ocean are so powerful that in a few seconds I can feel my soul, happy and energetic and ready to jump out of my body and swim.

2. Beneath the Blue

11

Getting used to productivity,
learning to move with the music,
trying to love,
accepting failures.
Alluring skies,
and wistful beaches.
There is so much left to explore,
but we remain lost in the world of *routine.*

12

If you ask me,
my art is in capturing,
often with words,
more often with pictures,
those moments when I felt real,
those moments when nothing felt real,
combining that feeling with my favourite song,
one with guitar riffs i'll never forget,
And I am transported into the frames,
reminiscing, thinking about,
all the cigarettes shared,
the laughter that filled rooms,
and the stories that make me human.
If the feelings of nostalgia were ever bottled,
I would be hooked.

13

Words and emotions,

flow out of me,

but I still feel like an open book that has been gathering dust,

the pages haven't been flipped over in weeks,

the spine begging to be held,

and the words yearning to be read by a kind eye.

But as this chapter comes to its end,

not a bone in my body wishes this book to shut.

Contrary to my first beach visit, we recently visited Goa again. I was so excited about wanting to sit on the shore and write poetry, I forgot that my love for the water ruled my mind. For not a second was I on the shore. I ran into the water and did not stop, my uncle and cousins following me. They warned me to stop when it got too deep and even though I had no desire to, I did. The feeling of just being in the water was so euphoric, I could not get enough. My mother was extremely scared for me, she thought I would drown, but I believed then, and still do that the ocean will never let anything happen to me. Finally we had to come back home. Part of me was very upset that we had to return, the only thing I wanted was to be back in the water. But part of me was also excited to write the poetry that my brain had thought of and bottled all these days.

3. Waves Woven with Memory

14

Summer at grandma's

waking up early and bathing first thing in the morning,

"Diya, dont forget to wash your hair!"

walking to the temple, hand in hand.

Empty stomach, little diya is more than happy to receive the prasadam.

Later, pampered by her grandmother's pazhampuris and vadas,

little diya's stomach was now fully satisfied.

Spending her afternoons running around the house sneakily,

as her ammama sleeps.

Playing with the spinning top she had made for her out of a baby coconut,

Diya found herself in the veranda.

The sun did not bother her,

although she was sweating.

"Diya!" her ammama shouts from the kitchen.

Into the shower,

she is once more forced, and evening is upon her.

It is now she remembers her parents back home and misses them.

Her ammama does not let her dwell for even a second,

after her nightly ten minute phone call with amma and acha,

Ammama tells her the story of the aana and the papaan*,

one she has long memorised.

but will listen to, with no complaints, every night.

*Elephant and Mahout

15

My childhood home,

greets you with a tall mango tree.

My childhood home,

where the evening primrose,

blooms on starry nights.

My childhood home,

where *it* first happened.

The walls of my home,

watched as you did *this deed.*

These walls,

have their eyes painted over with a bright yellow today,

These walls that once stared as you violated me,

have been stripped of that memory.

If only, the eyes in my mind could be painted yellow.

The swing that once hung from the neem tree,

is long gone.

The scribbles of chalk on the gates,

that were there every day, without fail,

are erased forever,

and there is nobody to scribble on them now.

My childhood bedroom,

Now lies empty.

I see the door shut tightly,

as though it may never be open again,

perhaps for the best.

The door of horrors in my mind,

has a striking similarity to this one,

and it runs red with blood.

16

These walls,

are closing in, closing in

who would have thought,

that their bleak grey colour,

would one day become the only thing that brings me comfort.

As my tears flow,

and my breathing becomes slower,

I am numb.

I can no longer feel my face or arms.

this pain in my chest,

has it always been there?

Certainly not when I was younger,

Right?

yet, I could not remember a time in my life where it wasn't a part of

me.

Could it be that when I had my innocence snatched from me,

It left me shattered forever?

It can't be,

Right?

Have I always carried all this weight?

Certainly not when I was a happy child, right?

Right?

Was I a happy child?

As John Lennon continues to sing to me,

I burn these thoughts away,

and bury their ashes,

far far away.

17

My Chicago,

my home and hiraeth.

the droplet of an ocean of memories,

bittersweet moments.

A home that will forever remain a home,

where the sunsets are irreplaceable,

where I encountered a mirage of thorn,

but also the most angelic roses.

A place where time never slowed.

and when I'm back in this city,

the sun doesn't set.

My Chigaco,

my home and hiraeth, where my smile does not fade,

where a version of me that knew love resides,

a place that will only ever be buried with memories.

4. Tides of Pain and Grief

18

Our scars tell different stories,

oftentimes not the story we want them to tell.

Scars glorify mistakes, accidents.

Scars don't belong, which is why they are so stubborn to leave.

Scars are normally applauded, they are called beacons of bravery.

What if they were residues of cowardice?

A reminder of the job you could not finish.

Emptiness.

Why do I feel so empty?

Sometimes, I feel as empty as those teacups set aside for guests.

Waiting, yearning,

only to be filled with hot tea and sipped by a stranger.

20

My Hair,

no matter how long or short it has been,

has always been my shield.

My shoulders, so broad.

it is a shame I still hide them.

My back, unyielding,

it stood tall through every blow and blade,

even when they came all at once.

My face,

learned how to smile through the pain, the tears and the blood.

Today, I am ready to take on a thousand more blows,

and a hundred more blades.

My body is no longer a body,

it is an armour, a warrior and a warcry, all in one.

21

Across this sea of madness,

I swim past the tides of horror.

Across the shore,

over the coastline,

something awaits.

I swim with the sharks,

my tears, salted with sorrow,

have vanished into the brine of the sea,

something seemed to be concealing the smell of my blood from the

sharks.

Or maybe, I have bled so much,

that even the sharks spared my life.

Maybe, in their pity,

even the sharks believed that I deserved to reach this shore.

22

Ideas for a burning poem,
words spilling out of me,
I'm riding at an all time high.
Existing with this pain is close to
psychotic torture,
so I set free,
with pure hatred.
Holding onto nothingness,
swimming in sorrow,
my body is breaking,
but I still move.
I cry into a cesspool of thoughts,
swimming in sorrow,
my soul is crushing,
but I still love.

23

Notes of cheap whiskey on my breath,

anybody but myself,

I wish I was anybody,

anybody but myself.

Notes of cheaper cigarettes on my breath,

I'm finally liking this version of myself,

I still wish I was anybody,

anybody but myself.

Years of abuse,

linger on my skin.

every second of the pain I endured,

has resurfaced,

I wish I was anybody,

anybody but myself.

Is this torture?

It must be.

Floating in this limbo of sobriety,

or is it an ocean of intoxication?

Will I ever let go?

Let go of memories past,

let go of the pain you caused.

But how am I to let go if every night,

when my eyes are shut I feel your hands all over me again?

I wish I was anybody,

anybody but myself.

I see the love,

I see it in your eyes,

Will I shatter this illusion you have of me?

Or let it go on for a moment longer than it should have,

I see how you want to continue to love me,

but will I let you?

I wish I was anybody,

anybody but myself,

Forever roaming this limbo of sobriety.

What does sobriety have to do with what I am feeling?

You said you'd see through it all,

but I should have realised no one signs up for an addict,

an addict or a woman,

am I an addict or just another woman?

Lost in this limbo of sobriety,

I am lucky if I am even human.

I wish I was anybody,

anybody but myself.

24

Four of us, sitting in this expensive restaurant,
there's sushi on the table, none of us reaching for it.
Sitting under a cloud of smoke,
one of us, decides to break the silence,
"Cheers" *clink*.
Tangled in a web of abuse, four of us,
sitting in this expensive restaurant,
there's beer on the table,
"Cheers" *clink*.

25

I am not trying to hurt anybody but myself.
"Go through it sober"
I strive to remember, I survive cach day,
so I can remember.
Why I am the way that I am,
what injustices have occurred,
and why I need to fix them?
Do you have the answer,
oh father, oh father?
Right, you never do.
"Go through it sober" yeah, I did.
I didn't start drinking till last year.
"Go through it sober" I think I already have,
years before my first drink.
"Go through it sober,"
mama, have a drink, and put your gun down.

26

I scream and I scream,

as if underwater, my voice does not travel.

All I want is to be left, to drown.

I want to scream again, this time,

the voice does not even reach my lips.

The sky above me was dark,

the luminous depths below me,

I did not even notice.

Darkness all around me, I float, and I float.

January

I felt like things were changing, and they did.

I was a weak mind put into a weak body.

And worst of all, I was expected to succeed.

I felt heavy,

which is funny, because all I did was starve.

skipping meals and smoking cigarettes,

lonely days and even lonelier nights.

My only recreation?

Intoxication, naturally.

I fell into an ocean of addiction,

and somehow managed to make it out alive.

5. Love that is Seabound

27

What is a poem if nothing but a song that bleeds from a romantic's
heart?
Words that have lingered deep inside us,
find their escape through poetry.
Love, heartbreak and melancholy all find their home in a poet's soul.
What is a poem if nothing but a rendition of a poet's tears?

28

Our small conversations keep me up at night,
blushing , making me feel like a crazy person.
Maybe it is the December air
and you are the christmas I am waiting for.
You are as sweet as sugar,
and everything nice.
Your dimples are little pools of happiness,
and I could swim in them for hours.

29

A girl in love,

in love with a boy who is sunshine and smiles,

A sad poet,

in love with a yellow sunflower.

A black cat,

in love with the moon.

30

I think *'love'* is what a lot of us spend our whole lives looking for,

I think about *love* a lot and how much it has to do with our existence,

a lot of us like to deny the fact that *love* indeed plays a huge part in our

lives,

I was one of them too,

but to what extent can a poet deny that *love* does cross her mind.

Love is in poetry and poetry is in *love*.

There is beauty in making words come alive with *love*,

there is beauty in making someone feel *loved*,

there is beauty in feeling *loved*.

It feels like all I think about, write about

is *love*.

How this sudden change became of me I do not know,

maybe the romantic in me finally met the poet,

and fell in *love*.

6. Weeping in the Undertow

31

Summer wine,

my eyes grew heavy,

as I watched you leave, heard you lie.

my eyes grew heavy,

my heart fell into my gut,

as I realised you will never love me the way I did you.

Were they right? when they warned me? but you walked in with such

ease,

peered into my soul, polluted it,

and stole my summer wine.

32

Oh leader of the crestfallen,

you have watched me beg and weep,

pray and scream.

Oh leader of the crestfallen,

won't you blind me? pluck out my eyes,

for these tears are growing too heavy.

Oh leader of the crestfallen,

let me fall in love blindly,

so I am immune to the pain of heartbreak.

Oh leader of the crestfallen,

Release me from the clutches of hope,

let my ruins be eaten by the vultures of love.

33

They bested me,

I tried time and again to fight,

but they got the best of me.

• 40 •

Oh leader of the crestfallen,

Must I be the one at loss?

After all these years,

Have you found no other crone,

No other poet whose eyes you may pluck?

Do I not deserve to see without this mist that blinds me?

34

My tears build up as deep as oceans,

salty just the same.

Begging all the gods whose existence I question everyday,

to let me live another day.

"Maybe I just need a good one to stay"

35

We are floating in unrequity,

there is no tomorrow for us in this city.

Crashing and burning,

falling and drowning,

Would you catch me?

Or would you stand there watching?

Are you the crone,

here to return my heart,

or will you fly away,

and leave me to the shadows?

Crashing and burning,

falling and drowning,

I stand still,

as I watch you, finally fly away.

My heart still bleeds,

as you clutch it between your sharp beak,

and the drops of blood that fall,

create pools of sorrow in its place.

And I still stand,

watching,

and I do not dare move a finger.

36

I fought for what we had,

I keep fighting to have those fleeting moments,

just hoping you would hold me tight one day.

Why don't you stay another night?

we will lose all track of time,

lay next to each other,

watch as time goes by and remain tucked under the blanket all evening.

I am holding out hope that one day my words come true into our reality,

one where I am blushing and your head is on my shoulder.

And we'll smell like each other for eternity.

37

Skies and stars apart,

fallen angels cry for you,

In this abyss of lovelessness and emptiness,

we found each other, dying.

I would give you my last breath,

my last loving bone would break for you.

Rotting, sneering and holding my breath with yours.

Time and again we have met in this limbo of heartbreak.

The world we dream of, where the grass is always green,

where we do not have to die to be together,

where our love is embraced and not caged,

it seems so far fetched.

Why are we so lonely in this loveless world when we have so much love

to give?

38

Sweet, sweet candy.

sour, sour tongues.

Red and blue,

became purple.

And when that purple began to turn into black,

I never noticed.

39

Use your heart, imagine lies,

kissing goodnight, hands intertwined.

Use your mind, imagine a life,

studio, big city, you and I.

Use your heart, imagine lies,

smoking cigarettes at 2 AM, on the fire escape.

New York skyline,

and glasses of wine.

Sunsets at Central Park,

you in jean shorts, laying on the dry grass.

Use your mind, imagine a life.

Imagine a life,

imagine a life where this is true,

a life where I do not die before 25,

a life where I would breathe without panting,

a life in which you are mine and I am yours.

The world is on our shoulders,

but you still carry us.

Use your heart, imagine lies,

lies better than reality,

lies you love hearing,

and lies I love telling.

40

Like twin flames,
in the middle of winter,
as the cold night breeze passes us,
with the flash of a light,
a sound in the distance,
for a quarter of a second,
neither of us was escaping.
Cold freezing mornings,
cloudy skies and a melancholic mist in the air,
this winter morning,
I bleed through the cracks on my lips.
I watched the sunrise,
and packed my bags.
And like twin flames,
We separated.

Mid July, City Lights
My room is now black,
the walls are now stripped,
stripped of their memories,
stripped clean.
Did I paint them black?
Taint them with my tears?
Crack the walls with my screams?
Last july,
you were here,
and we looked at the city lights.
I suppose the cracks were there even then,
we were so lost in the world inside our heads,
that I never noticed what was outside of it.

7. Seafoam and Solitude

41

I wonder,
what made us scribble when we were younger,
and why was it looked at as primeval?
Am I not scribbling while writing this?
No, no how could you say that?
this is poetry, fool.

42

I am standing on my balcony,
as I have stood many nights before,
but today I think of different things,
I think of poetry,
I think of art,
and I think of who decides which art is good,
which poem is not articulate enough,
Why must it be anyway?
Can't art remain art,
and poetry remain poetry?
This world,
built by us people, only exists
to question the art and the artists.
We crave freedom so much,
how can we seek freedom when we,
ourselves, built the cage?
I believe that there are people in this world who see everything through
a lens,
and that there are people that question the very existence of the lens.
I also believe that there are people who choose to close their eyes,
and those are the people that live the most peaceful lives.

43

Poets are martyrs of love,
yearning, searching and seeking for a glimpse,
a whiff of home, of comfort, of love.
Hurting, drained and slowly withering,
clutching that glimmer of hope ever so tightly.
but a martyr is only a martyr after he is dead.
poets will never fully die,
yet they will be martyrs of what they could never conquer.
A part of us will always live on through our art,
our pain will not be forgotten,
and our heartache will be felt by many more poets to come.

44

Emotional and lucid,

I imagine that is what death would feel like,

death has no place in reality,

because anyone that knows what it feels like,

is not here to say so.

Thoughts of death and suicide

crawl in a man's brain

like worms in soil,

digging deeper and deeper.

Is the judgement of the body,

as good as the mind's?

Can one even trust their own mind?

Mother and crone,

Father, Son and the Holy Ghost.

Here comes the angel of death,

In your disguise.

Guiding the worms in our minds,

to their final resting place.

45

This strange storm,

has been brewing for days,

nights filled with lightning and rage,

but as I look up to the sky,

which is full of long white cracks,

shaking with a current so full of sorrow,

I feel more empty than ever.

I watch,

as the rain drops fall, one by one,

I look at each drop of water,

my gaze is rather apologetic.

The water begins to rise around me,

and the storm grew louder,

this time,

the storm felt real,

and I wondered,

if I would rise from it all.

In that moment, I felt nothing but fear

and agony over my possible demise.

Did I really want to die?

From this storm too,

I emerged.

The water around me is still,

the waves are silent.

the sky is ever so cloudy,

but there is no rain.

My tears have been wiped,

and I continue to stare in silence,

a taste of peace,
oh, so sweet.

Loss

I found myself saying to myself *"I've lost a lot in this life"*

it's true, I did.

I've lost friends, loved ones, and even myself.

The hardest to get back certainly being the latter,

as I'm sure is no surprise to anyone,

all the songs and poems talk about losing and finding yourself.

"I've lost a lot in this life"

but, when i lost myself,

I lost the very essence of life,

I lost all the reasons I had to breathe on this earth,

I lost the confidence that others had in me,

I lost the charm that made others smile,

and I lost the art that had made its home in me.

That one hurt the most.

"*I've lost a lot in this life*"

Everyone assumes that loss is the hard part,

It was.

but I had to fight tooth and nail,

fight tooth and nail with an enemy that anticipated my every next

move.

As I kept fighting,

I began to find the wit that that was once erased from my mind,

I found the skill that enriched my art,

And like the evening primrose under the moonlight,

My soul began to bloom, slowly but surely:

"I've lost a lot in this life"

My losses might be in thousands,

and my soul only one,

but it fights, tooth and nail,
to bloom fully under the moonlight.

Fin.

As this version of *seascapes* ends,

A part of my life has concluded,

These poems,

Written over the years,

Are an undeiable part of me,

A piece of my heart.

9 798889 295492